Midnight Musings
of a Muddled Mind

D. Elizabeth

BookLeaf Publishing

India | USA | UK

Presentation by *BookLeaf Publishing*

Web: www.bookleafpub.com

E-mail: info@bookleafpub.com

ISBN: 9789357449892

First edition 2022

DEDICATION

Grandpa,

This one's for you. I wouldn't be who I am without you. Even though you insist you're "sour 15 and never been kissed" I sure am glad you had a kid, who had kid, who got to grow up with a rascal like you.

I love you most.

ACKNOWLEDGEMENT

There's so many people in my life who have helped me get to this moment. I could create a book with merely their names. In the interest of concision and anonymity, I won't.

Cat Lady, you're my rock. My giant, sometimes ridiculous, rock. Thank you for investing in me. I love you.

My Co- you quickly became an irreplaceable part of my life. Thank you for all your help with this collection, for being the 'co' I never knew I needed, and for loving me- even after you learned I was a yolk.

My oldest (but youngest) best friend, you're the person I've loved the longest, making you the love of my life and the first member of my chosen family. I wouldn't be here without you. Thank you for being you, and for growing up with me.

My Witchy Wife, thank you for teaching me, for loving me, for accepting me. You're brilliant, and I'm so thrilled to have you in my life. I really do pick the best 'wives'.

And Keli Jackson, the greatest Wise Wizard this world has ever seen. Sure, 'Life Coach' might be a professional title, but you're the sage mentor I needed to meet on my quest. So much in my life has changed for the better since I started your program. For everything you've taught me, and for being such an incredible human, I thank you.

PREFACE

As are the thoughts that we lie awake pondering, some of these poems are light and silly, while others take a darker turn. It would be inauthentic of me to exclude them from this collection. That said, for anyone in a dark, or dim, state. Check out the third poem in this book; then get some rest.

Love,

D. Elizabeth

Writing Della

I'm on a quest–
an adventure, if you will–
I search for myself,
what it is to be real.

Plant Mom Life

Some people leave the house
wondering if they left their oven on.
Not me.
No.
I lie awake at three in the morning
fighting the urge to go
check that I actually
watered my plants this week,
or if they're growing,
or wilting, or
getting enough
sunlight
.

.

.

Is this what parenthood is like?

I Lo-lo-lo-lo-love You

Yeah, You.
You, reading this right now.

Some say that using those three little words
'too often'
causes them to lose their impact.
As though there will be
a stock market crash
that brings the world to a screeching halt.
All because people
Love
without reason–
or with
reckless abandon.

I don't know about You,
but my Great Depression,
had nothing to do
with too much "I Love You."
In fact,
It's what I craved most.
And I never,

Never Ever,
Never
Ever
Ever
EV-
-ER
want someone else to feel that way.

So,
I Love You.
No one can take that away from You.
It's mine to give,
and I've chosen You.

You, when you're joyous.
You, when you smile.
You, when you talk about your passions.
You, when you're just existing.
You, when you're sad,
Or lonely.

You, thinking about this later.
You, unable to sleep.
You, when you're embarrassed.
You, when you feel unlovable.
You, when you have no one,
Or think you have no one.

I love you.

Personalities

I took a personality test and
Now I understand why I had trouble
Finding people who really get me. If
Just 1.5% of the world is like me

—

Assuming that number is correct- I hit the
jackpot with my little group of friends.

Five of twenty-one
of my slated
poems have been done.

I anticipated none,
yet here I have created
five of twenty-one!

I feared I'd not get them done
and felt infuriated
before I'd even begun.

I've truly had such great fun
writing these- the fated
five of twenty-one.

I can't wait to show everyone
that these long-awaited
poems have been done.

This gap should only be one line- why is it so
large?

I feel like I've finally won–
I'm immensely elated–
even while only five of twenty-one
poems have been done.

26

Twenty-six
hit me like a ton
of bricks.
Thus begun
my youth's eclipse.

Is 27 too young to be senile? Asking for a friend.

I like awake wondering, "What rhymes with
twenty-seven?"
This poem can't be written without answering
the question!
Every year I commemorate
the years since my birth date
But all that comes to mind is f*cking 'Kevin'!

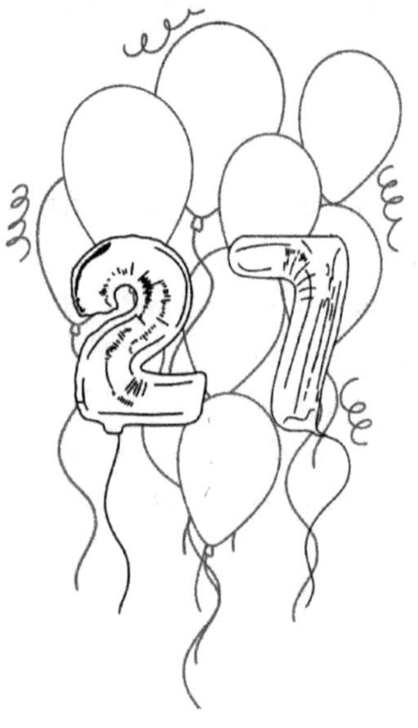

Hyper-fixation Haiku x2

Hyper-fixation
leads you down a rabbit hole
every time you try

to research something.
So, what I'm saying is; seals
have hidden fingers.

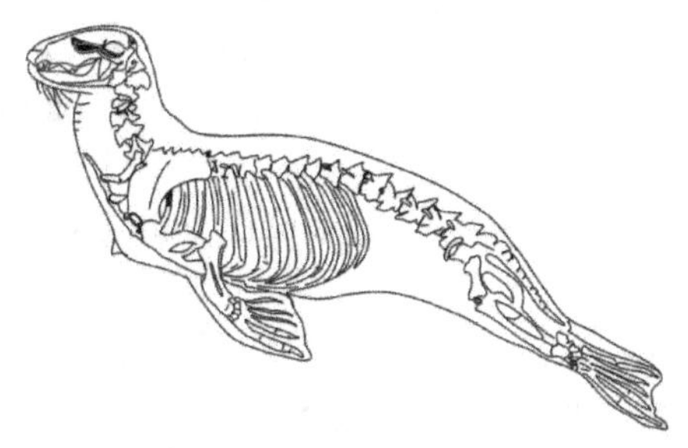

2:49 am

I've lain awake every night this week,
lost moments racing through my mind,
recounting the events in my schedule
wondering where I'll find the time
to make everyone happy, and just
wishing I could get some sleep.

Oh, how I miss sleep!
I remember all the days I'd have time
to rest and relax, just
enjoy the upcoming week–
forget about the schedule
and appointments– and let peace fill my mind.

Nowadays I feel like I'm losing my mind.
Clock *tick-tock*-ticking down seconds, taking my
time,
meetings, no, should-be-emails flooding my
schedule
bringing anxiety to ravage my sleep
as I beg Father Time to just
let me be this week.

After all, he already stole last week
from me. He ransacked my mind

as I yearned for sleep,
bringing up panic from the last time
I couldn't keep up and just
completely botched my schedule.

My, I'm so sick of this schedule!
So many rules and dates, and so little time
it makes me sick when it fills my mind!
If only I could get good sleep,
enough to get through an entire week,
I'd feel so energized and just–

get so many things done and just–
breathe. For once, invite serenity to mind
forget about the schedule
and all the deadlines and due time
I'd get so much sleep
if only I could have a clear week.

That's just what's on my mind
as I reset my sleep schedule,
for the seventh time this week.

Imposter Syndrome

You ever lie awake
in the wee hours,
wondering,
panicking,
"Oh my everything...
Am I a fraud?"

I do.

I tell people I write,
and crochet,
and sew,
and draw,
and even sculpt clay.

(I do.)

But then *they think*
that I can write
and crochet
and sew,
and draw,
and even sculpt clay.

And that's terrifying.

Ominous Positivity

When you feel alone,
or like no one really cares,
just remember that
there are cryptids everywhere
rooting for you in shadows.

Exchanging Pleasantries I

People are hurting,
it's plain to see. What I can't
seem to grasp is why,
when someone asks how they are,
do the broken say they're fine?

Exchanging Pleasantries II

I try my best to
hide the pain even while I'm
yearning for someone
to see through me when I say,
"I'm fine, thanks, have a good day."

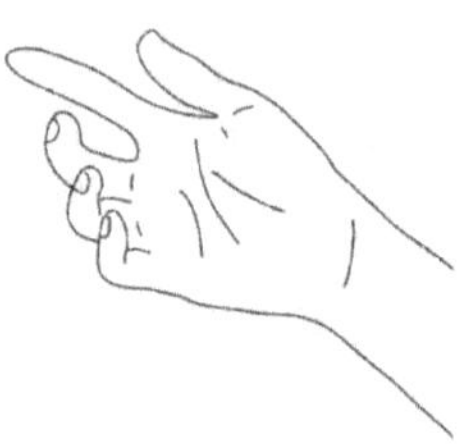

Trigger Warnings in Mourning

Memories plague me
as I try to rest my eyes.
The monsters still lurk
in the abyss of my mind,
haunting, my innocence lost

Anxiety and Ancestral Curses

All I can seem to think about is the
Next thing that can go wrong, like that
Xenophobic groups will further spread their hate and
Instill bigotry in the hearts of children, and the world will fall into
Exclusion and seclusion, and everything will be on fire, all
The while you say, "That won't happen, calm down."
Yet I wonder how you can look at the state of this country and
    not see that
        Our ancestors started it–
          Built and cultivated it,
            This system from which *we*
benefit
             that perpetuates it,
    not so long ago?

Panic Attack

I used to think
panic attacks were
hyperventilating,
weeping,
gasping for air.

Sure,
sometimes they are.
For me, though,
they're more like

talking so fast I can barely keep up–
hands shaking like a chilly chihuahua–
laughter laced with hysteria,
and hiding it all the best I could.

Of course,
I didn't know
I was having panic attacks;
it was just daily life.

Maybe, though
if we all worked together,
we could educate each other
to create communities

where most everyone can
recognize the signs.

Then maybe, just maybe,
we can all begin understand
mental health
just a little bit better.

Rewritten

The most powerful thing
I've ever done
is take a
good,
hard
look
at who I was becoming,
and start over.

I'm the person now
that I've always wanted to be,
the person I needed when I was a teen,
I wouldn't be
if I hadn't looked at
the story I was writing
with my life and
decided it needed to be
rewritten.

Nice is a Knock-Off

I'm not a fan of nice.
It lacks depth and sincerity.

Kindness is truth.
It's the hard conversations,
it's really considering your words.
it's growing from the
dark
hard
awful places
to bring beauty to others;

like a rose bush
outside a jail.
So pretty,
so frail.

Nice is,
"You always look great,"
when the truth is often more like,
"Sometimes you look like a trash goblin
who never learned what a bath was,
and I love you all the while."
Which is way better,
I think.

What if you can?

We often allow our thoughts to wreck
Havoc on our dreams and
Aspirations as
Though failure is the only possible outcome.

In shifting our perspectives,
Fantasies come alive!

Your wildest dreams are
Out there waiting for you to
Uppercut your fears and

Create the reality you have
Always hoped for; and there's
No better time to start, than now!

Echoes

A Wise Wizard
taught me when we panic
over what people think,
it's not because
we're afraid they believe it.
It's because
we already do.
If friends and strangers believe it,
that will make it true.

We fear they echo our own self-deprecating
thoughts.
Thus it will be writ in stone as fact.

So when I walk into caves
to shout my thoughts
waiting to be carved
in the stone of my mind,
I stopped yelling;
"You're too big!
"You're not pretty enough"
"You'll never succeed!"
I quit waiting for my venom to echo back to me.

And started cheering,

"You're a human being!"
"You're a person deserving of basic human
decency!"
and
"You can build anything with the right tools and
foundation!"

And that
neutrality
feels a whole lot better
than all that
hate.
It's let me stair-step my way
from the aggression of
"I hate myself,"
to the shock and awe of,
"I think I love myself."

Beginning at the End

If this
poem exists in
this book,
In this published work
that Someone, Somewhere,
Spent their time reading…

Maybe I can write.
And maybe you can do whatever you do, too.

Maybe hurdling over those first
chasms and hills at the beginning
is actually the hardest part.
Maybe it never really was
about good enough, but
instead, it's about
getting past
Start.

Additionally, why is this gap so large? The other images are directly under text, or spaced by a different section?

9 789357 449892